Table of Contents
Spelling Homework Booklet
Grade 2

Bale Them Up 2
Keep the Beat 4
A Mine Find 6
Coasting Along 8
Parachuting 10
Now Docking 12
Don't Be Stumped 14
Camping Out 16
Review 18
Off to the Market 20
Twirling and Whirling 22
Sliding into Home 24
A Treasure Trunk 26
Fill In the Blanks 28
What a Shine! 30
Reach for These 32
Looking Good 34
Showering Clouds 36
Review 38
On the Double 40
Awesome Animals 42
Have Another One 44
A Magical Compound 46
Composing Compounds 48
Write It Right! 50
Pick a Pair of Pears 52
Review 54
Don't Be Confused 56
A Family Gathering 58
A Circus of Colors 60
The Countdown Begins 62
Cool Choices 64
What a Busy Day 66
'Tis the Season for Holidays 68
Review 70

©1992 Instructional Fair, Inc.

Bale Them Up

Word List

bait, safe, trail, pay, mail, way, plate, rake, age, day, pain, hay

Write the **ai** words that make the /ā/ sound.

_____   _____
_____   _____

Write the **ay** words that make the /ā/ sound.

_____   _____
_____   _____

Write the words ending with **e** that make the /ā/ sound.

_____   _____
_____   _____

Write the letters that make the /ā/ sound.

_____   _____   _____

/ā/

Read each sentence. Use the Word List to write the missing word in the boxes.

1. Please put the ___ on the table.
2. Which ___ do we go now?
3. Robin likes to ___ the leaves.
4. Todd put the coins in the ___.
5. He could read by the ___ of six.
6. Ben put the ___ on the hook.
7. The horses will eat the ___.
8. They will ___ a dime for the pony ride.
9. We like to hike the ___ to the lake.
10. It is a sunny ___.
11. Did I get a letter in the ___?
12. He felt a lot of ___ when he stepped on the nail.

©1992 Instructional Fair, Inc.   IF0126 Spelling

Keep the Beat

Word List

mean   feet
deep   meal
team   keep
each sweet tree
treat sneeze
leave

Write the double **e** words that make the /ē/ sound.

_____   _____
_____   _____
_____   _____

Write the **ea** words that make the /ē/ sound.

_____   _____
_____   _____
_____   _____

Write the letters that make the /ē/ sound.

_____   _____

/ē/

Read each sentence. Use the Word List to write the missing word.

1. We must _____ for school now.

2. The cake tastes very _____.

3. The water in the lake is very _____.

4. There is a balloon for _____ of us.

5. What can we eat for our _____?

6. The _____ dog barked at me.

7. After walking all the way home, his _____ were sore.

8. Rob is glad that he will be on Jeff's baseball _____.

9. When you have a cold, you sometimes _____ a lot.

10. Please _____ your desk neat.

11. The bird built a nest on a branch of the oak _____.

12. Ice cream is Irene's favorite _____.

A Mine Find

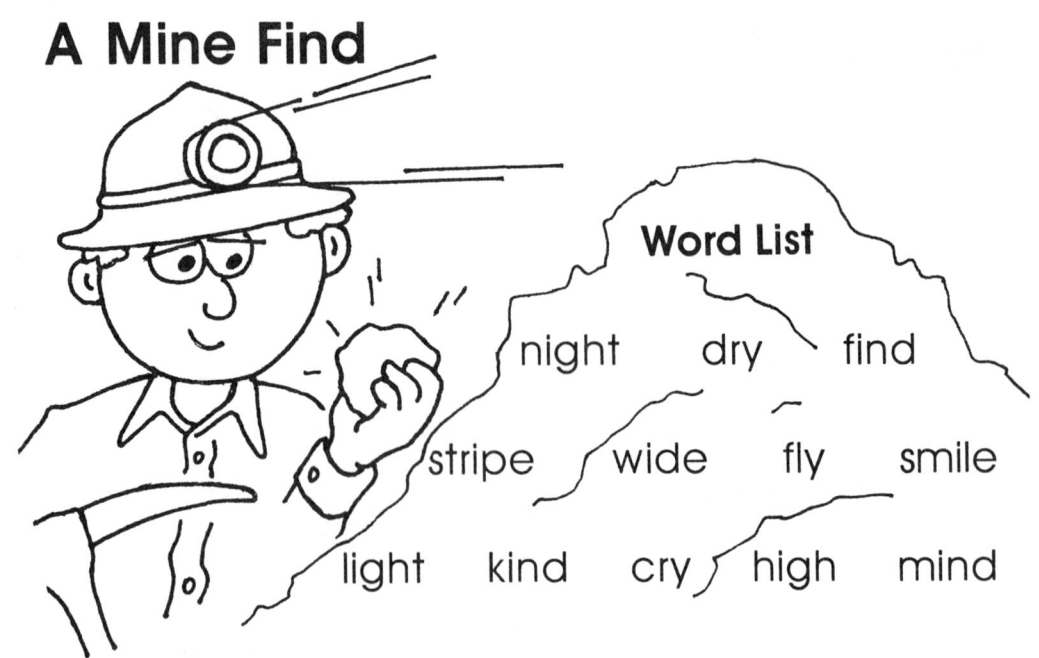

Word List: night, dry, find, stripe, wide, fly, smile, light, kind, cry, high, mind

Write the words ending with **e** that make the /ī/ sound.

_____ _____ _____

Write the **igh** words that make the /ī/ sound.

_____ _____ _____

Write the words ending with **y** that make the /ī/ sound.

_____ _____ _____

Write the words with **i** followed by **nd** that make the /ī/ sound.

_____ _____ _____

Read each clue. Write the correct word from the maze on each line. Then trace a path from the miner to his find in the same order as your answers.

1. Opposite of wet _____
2. Opposite of laugh _____
3. Opposite of mean _____
4. To obey your parents _____
5. Opposite of day _____
6. You do this when you are happy _____
7. Opposite of narrow _____
8. You need this to see in the dark _____
9. What a bird does _____
10. Not low, but... _____
11. A band of color _____
12. To discover _____

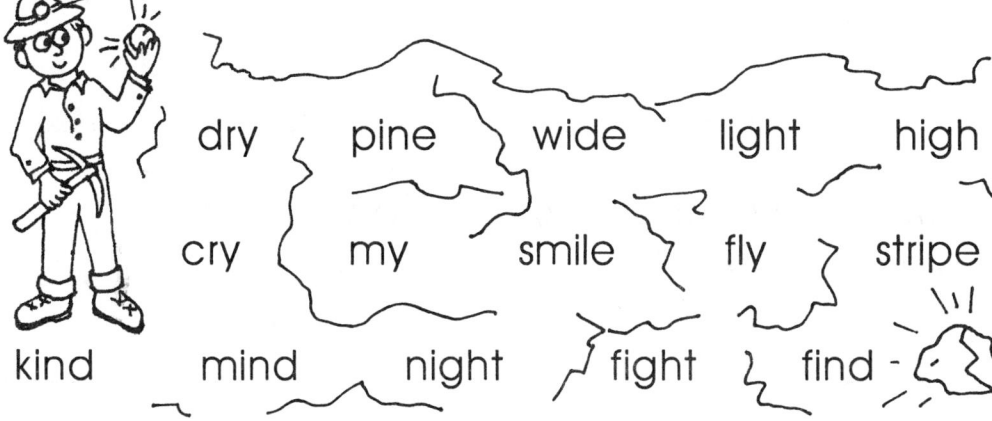

Coasting Along

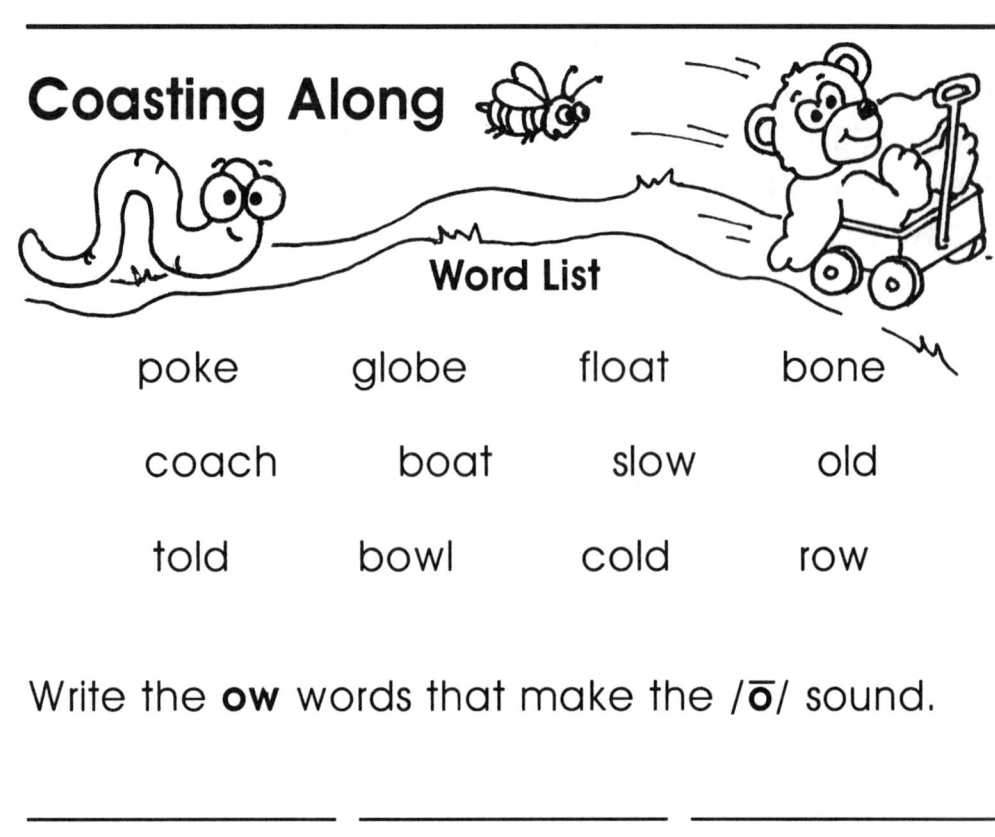

Word List

poke	globe	float	bone
coach	boat	slow	old
told	bowl	cold	row

Write the **ow** words that make the /ō/ sound.

_____ _____ _____

Write the **oa** words that make the /ō/ sound.

_____ _____ _____

Write the words ending with **e** that make the /ō/ sound.

_____ _____ _____

Write the words with **o** followed by **ld** that make the /ō/ sound.

_____ _____ _____

/ō/

Read each sentence. Use the Word List to write the missing word in the boxes.

1. We have a new ___ for our football team.
2. Mother ___ me to mow the grass.
3. Please put the oranges in a ___.
4. You can find the United States on a ___.
5. Jody gave her dog a ___.
6. It was so ___, the water froze.
7. My ___ coat has a hole in it.
8. Don't ___ your finger with the pin.
9. They will row the ___ across the lake.
10. There was so much traffic that we had to ___ down.
11. Put all of the chairs in one ___.
12. Will the raft ___ or sink?

Parachuting

Word List
tube
zoo   balloon   moon
boot   moose   food   tune
cool   rude   room   pool

Write the words ending with **e** that make the /ü/ sound.

_____ _____ _____

Write the double **o** words that make the /ü/ sound.

_____ _____ _____

_____ _____ _____

_____ _____ _____

Write the words that rhyme with these pictures.

_____ _____ _____

_____ _____

_____

/ü/

Read each clue. Use the Word List to write the words on the lines. Then use the numbered letters to solve the code.

1. A kind of flying toy   _ _ _ _ _ _
                                  1
2. You can sing it.   _ _ _ _
                                2
3. Opposite of warm   _ _ _ _
                          3
4. Like a hose or straw   _ _ _ _
                            4
5. A part of a house   _ _ _ _
                          5
6. A kind of shoe   _ _ _ _
                            6
7. An animal with antlers _ _ _ _ _
                                7
8. It shines at night.   _ _ _ _
                                8
9. You can swim in it.   _ _ _ _
                          9
10. Impolite    _ _ _ _
                                 10
11. What you eat   _ _ _ _
                          11
12. Where some animals live _ _ _
                                 12

_ _ _ _ _
7 4 9 2 5

_ _ _ _
3 6 12 1

_ _ _!
11 10 8

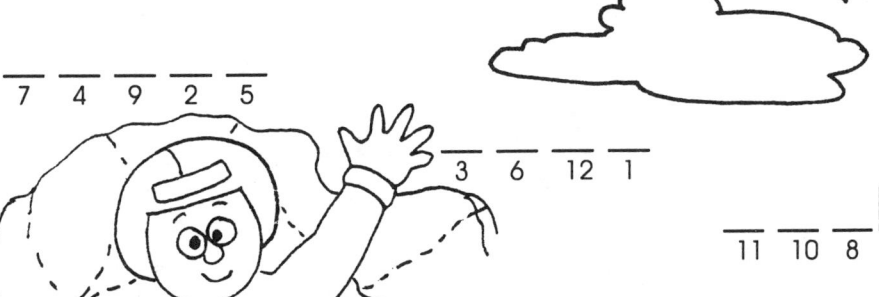

Now Docking

Word List

pick	cap	lock
clock	kick	pack
cost	flock	king
back	snack	sick

Write the words ending with **ck** that make the /**k**/ sound.

_____ _____ _____

_____ _____ _____

_____

Write the words beginning with **c** that make the /**k**/ sound.

_____ _____

Write the words beginning with **k** that make the /**k**/ sound.

_____ _____

Write the words ending with **ck** and beginning with **c** or **k** that make the /**k**/ sound.

_____ _____

c, k and ck

Write the words that rhyme with  .

_____   _____   _____

Write the words that rhyme with  .

_____   _____   _____

Write the words that rhyme with  .

_____   _____   _____

Read each clue. Use the Word List to write the correct word on the line. Then circle the words in the puzzle.

1. A kind of hat   _____
2. The price   _____
3. The ruler of a country _____
4. A group of geese   _____

c	o	s	t	f	k
f	l	o	c	k	i
l	t	c	o	c	n
o	s	p	i	a	g
c	k	a	k	p	c

Don't Be Stumped

Word List

desk	best	task
fast	stand	state
lost	ask	mask
stump	step	last

Write the words that begin like 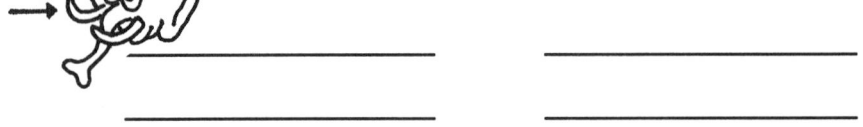 .

_____   _____

_____   _____

Write the words that end with the same sounds as 🐘 .

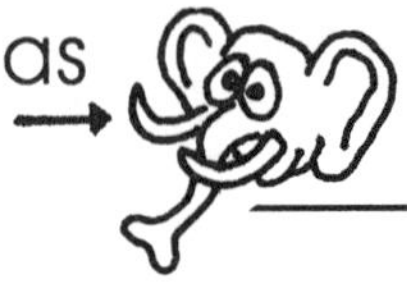

_____   _____

_____   _____

Write the words that end with the same sounds as 🪺 .

_____   _____

_____   _____

sk and st

Read each sentence. Use the Word List to write the missing word.

1. Beth _____ her new coat.
2. The chipmunk sat on the tree _____.
3. Dan wore a pirate _____ to the costume party.
4. Put your book on the _____.
5. Watch your _____ when you get off the bus.
6. She lives in the _____ of New York.
7. Steve can run very _____.
8. They were the _____ ones to leave the house.
9. If you _____ by the window, you can see the lightning.
10. Grandmother bakes the very _____ apple pie.
11. Stan must do a small _____ before he can play.
12. Did you _____ your cousin to go to the game?

Camping Out

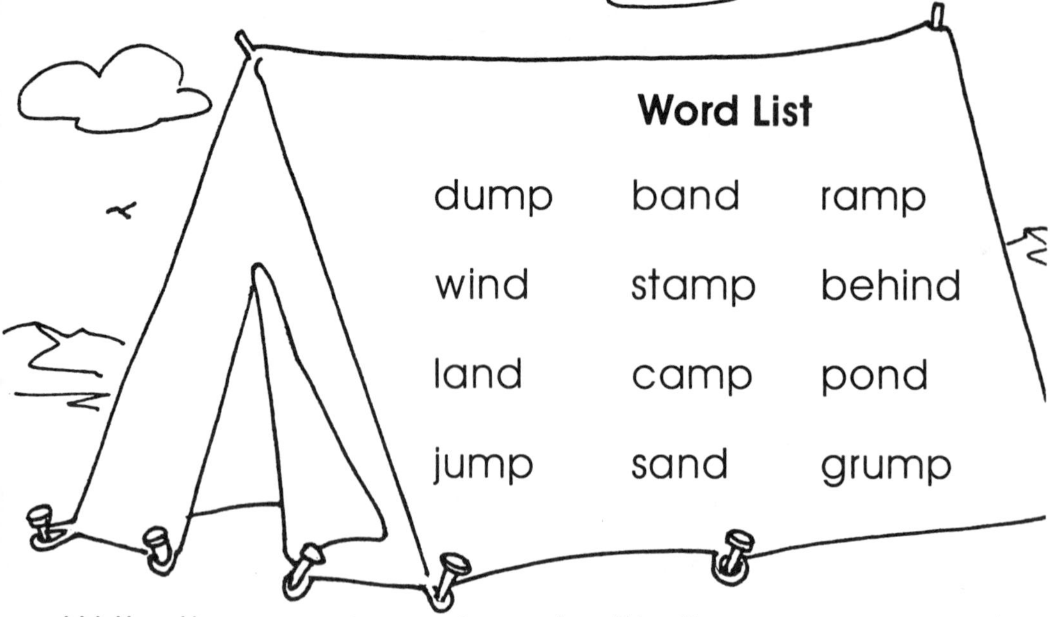

Word List

dump	band	ramp
wind	stamp	behind
land	camp	pond
jump	sand	grump

Write the words that end with the same sounds as _____ . _____ _____

_____ _____

_____ _____

Write the words that end with the same sounds as _____ . _____ _____

_____ _____

_____ _____

Write the words that rhyme with these pictures.

_____ _____ _____

_____ _____ _____

_____ _____ _____

mp and nd endings

Make sure you have everything for the perfect camping trip. Write the Word List words in alphabetical order.

1. _____
2. _____
3. _____
4. _____
5. _____
6. _____
7. _____
8. _____
9. _____
10. _____
11. _____
12. _____

Review

Pages 2-3 Write the /ā/ word that names each picture.

_____ _____

_____ _____

_____ _____

Pages 4-5 Use the letters to help spell the missing /ē/ words. Write the words on the lines.

ea   p m w n l t r s d   ee

1. Never be _____ to animals.
2. We planted a _____ in the backyard.
3. Chocolate cake tastes very _____.
4. Ted's _____ will play a big game today.
5. The big dog dug a _____ hole in the dirt.
6. Lunch is my favorite _____.

Pages 6-7 Write the /ī/ word that means the opposite.

day   _____
wet   _____
lose   _____
laugh   _____
narrow   _____
mean   _____
dark   _____
frown   _____

Pages 8-9 Circle all of the /ō/ words in the puzzle. Then write the words on the lines.

t	b	o	w	l	p	o	k	e
o	r	o	w	b	o	n	e	o
l	c	o	a	c	h	o	o	l
d	o	f	l	o	a	t	l	d

_____ _____
_____ _____
_____ _____
_____ _____

Pages 10-11 Unscramble the letters to spell /ü/ words. Write the words on the lines.

nomo _____   lnobola _____
rdeu _____   tobo _____
oloc _____   unte _____

Pages 12-17 Use the letters to finish each word. Then write the whole word on the line.

    ck   sk   st   nd   mp

1. The wi___ blew very hard. _____
2. Please put a sta___ on the letter. _____
3. Jake stood behi___ me in line. _____
4. Do not du___ that down the sink. _____
5. Carol looked everywhere for her lo___ kitten. _____
6. Please a___ me if you need help. _____
7. Missy will help pi___ the apples. _____
8. Harry put the books on the de___. _____
9. How fa___ can you run? _____
10. A flo___ of geese flew over the lake. _____

Off to the Market

Word List

cart	horse	far
dark	store	corn
start	for	morning
short	barn	large

Write the words with the same vowel sound as 🚗. Then circle the letters that make the sound.

_____ _____ _____

_____ _____ _____

Write the words with the same vowel sound as 🍴. Then circle the letters that make the sound.

_____ _____ _____

_____ _____ _____

Change the first letter(s) of each word to make a rhyming word. Use the letters:

    d   b   m   f   y

1. dark _____   4. short _____
2. barn _____   5. far _____
3. store _____   6. corn _____

/är/ and /ôr/

Proofread the story. Circle the misspelled words. Then write the words correctly on the lines.

Early in the merning Carmen went to the born. She hitched her hirse to the cort. Then she went far a shirt ride to the field. There she loaded the korn into the cart. Carmen started down the road with the larje load. The town was very fur away. At last she got to the stowre. After unloading the cart, she had to shart back to the farm before it got too derk.

_____   _____

_____   _____

_____   _____

_____   _____

_____   _____

Twirling and Whirling

Word List

herd	girl
shirt	jerk
her	germ
stir	skirt
first	clerk
dirt	hers

Write the words with **er** that make the sound you hear in the middle of 🌿 .

_____ _____ _____

_____ _____ _____

Write the words with **ir** that make the sound you hear in the middle of 🐦.

_____ _____ _____

_____ _____ _____

The letters **ur** can also make the same sound as **er** and **ir**. Follow the directions to make these words. The first one is done for you.

fern - f (+ b) - er (+ ur) + n = burn

her - h (+ f) - er (+ ur) = _____

dirt - d (+ h) - ir (+ ur) + t = _____

Use the Word List to complete the puzzles.

/û/

Across
1. Not his
3. Another word for blouse
5. To move suddenly

Down
1. A group of cows
2. Mix with a spoon
4. Opposite of him

Across
2. Not a boy, but a . . .
4. Something to wear
5. Another word for soil

Down
1. Worker in a store
2. Tiny organism that can cause disease
3. Opposite of last

Sliding into Home

Word List

sled	spark	space
speech	slow	spy
sleet	spoon	slide
slip	speed	slick

Write the words that begin like

_____ _____ _____

_____ _____ _____

Write the words that begin like .

_____ _____ _____

_____ _____ _____

Write the word that rhymes.

place _____   fry _____
beach _____   need _____
moon _____   drip _____
fed _____   ride _____
pick _____   dark _____
crow _____   feet _____

s blends

Read each clue. Use the Word List to write the words on the lines. Then use the numbered letters to solve the code.

1. To secretly watch   __ __ __
                                           1

2. Partly frozen rain   __ __ __ __ __
                                                 2

3. You eat soup with it.   __ __ __ __ __
                                                 3

4. A public talk   __ __ __ __ __ __
                                                 4

5. You play on it.   __ __ __ __ __
                                                 5

6. To trip and fall   __ __ __ __
                                              6

7. To drive too fast   __ __ __ __ __
                                           7

8. Very slippery   __ __ __ __ __
                                                8

9. Where stars exist   __ __ __ __ __
                                           9

10. You use it when it snows.   __ __ __ __
                                                10

11. A tiny flash of fire   __ __ __ __ __
                                              11

12. Opposite of fast   __ __ __ __
                                           12 13

__ __ u __   __ __ __ __ __ __
1 12   9 8 12 11 5 10

__ __ __   __ __ __ __ __ __ g
2 4 5   13 6 3 3 6 3

__ __ __ __ __ !
7 12 6 3 2

©1992 Instructional Fair, Inc.   IF0126 Spelling

A Treasure Trunk

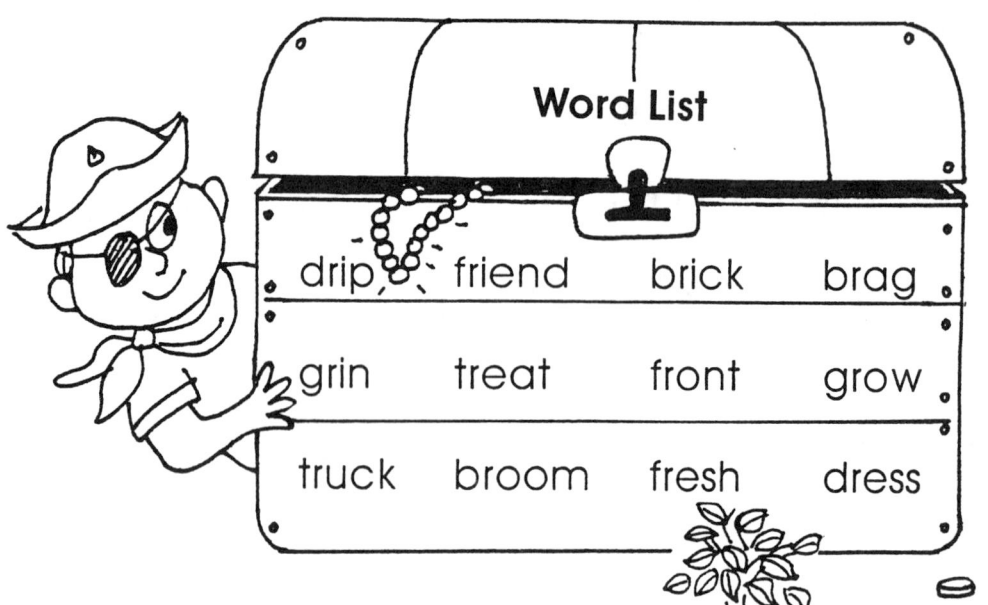

Write the words that begin like 🌳 .

_____   _____

Write the words that begin like  .

_____   _____

Write the words that begin like  .

_____   _____

Write the words that begin like  .

_____   _____

Write the words that begin like  .

_____   _____   _____

Read each clue. Write the correct word from the maze on each line. Then trace a path from the boat to the treasure trunk in the same order as your answers.

1. You sweep with it. _____
2. To get bigger _____
3. Something to wear _____
4. A kind of motor vehicle _____
5. Opposite of back _____
6. A leak in a water tap can do this. _____
6. Not stale _____
8. To smile _____
9. To boast _____
10. Some houses are made of this. _____
11. Trick or ___ _____
12. A person who likes you _____

front   drip   fresh   grin
drove
grab   brag
       truck   brick
              free   trip
broom   bright
grow   treat friend
       dress

Fill In the Blanks

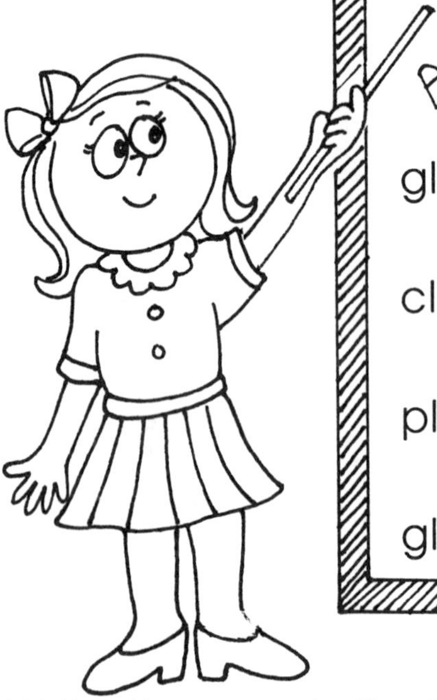

Word List

glue	blink	close
click	please	blast
plum	glass	plan
glad	blanket	clean

Write the words that begin like 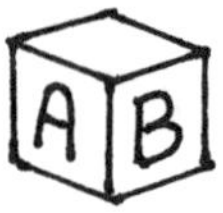 .

______________ ______________ ______________

Write the words that begin like .

______________ ______________ ______________

Write the words that begin like .

______________ ______________ ______________

Write the words that begin like .

______________ ______________ ______________

©1992 Instructional Fair, Inc.

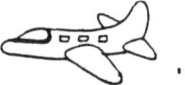

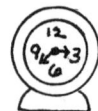

l blends

Read each sentence. Use the Word List to write the missing word.

1. Glenn asked, "May I _____ go play now?"

2. We live very _____ to a park.

3. Would you like a ripe _____ to eat?

4. The loud _____ of the firecracker scared us.

5. Do they _____ to visit their aunt?

6. Blain can _____ the broken vase back together.

7. Karen put a new _____ on her bed.

8. Please bring me a _____ of iced tea.

9. John was _____ he passed the test.

10. The bright light made me _____ my eyes.

11. We must _____ up this mess.

12. You hear a _____ when you push the button.

What a Shine!

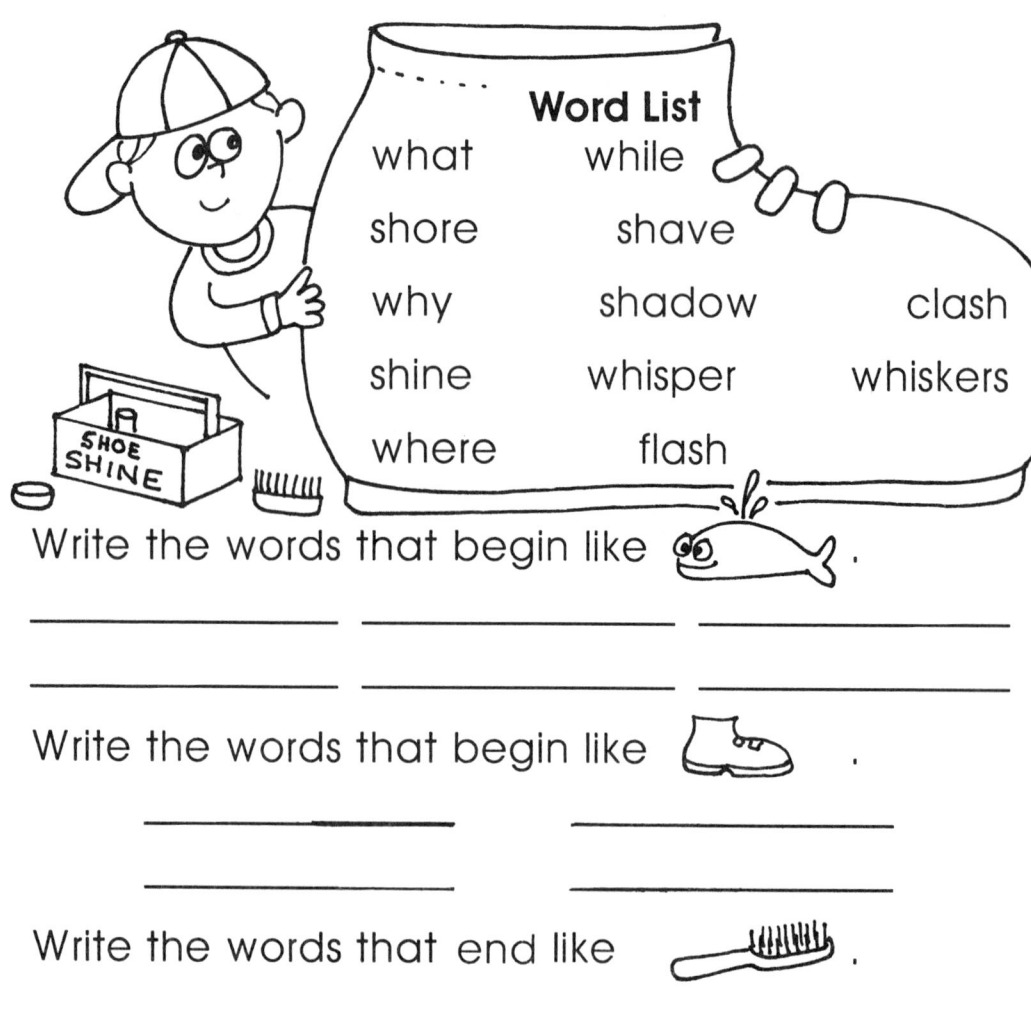

Word List

what   while
shore shave
why   shadow   clash
shine whisper   whiskers
where flash

Write the words that begin like 🐋 .

_____   _____   _____

_____   _____   _____

Write the words that begin like 👟 .

_____   _____

_____   _____

Write the words that end like 🖌 .

_____   _____

Challenge! Write as many rhyming words as you can.

1. clash _____
2. shave _____
3. why _____
4. while _____

sh and wh

Read each sentence. Circle the misspelled words. Then write the words correctly on the lines.

1. We found seashells wile walking along the chore.
2. The cat cleaned its wiskers.
3. Wy did he save off his beard?
4. Did you see the flach of lightning?
5. Please wisper in the library.
6. That shirt will clach with these pants.
7. You can see your shado on a sunny day.
8. Were is the kitten hiding?
9. Wut was his name?
10. Will the sun chine today?

_____   _____

_____   _____

_____   _____

_____   _____

_____   _____

_____   _____

Reach for These

Word List

chore　think　each
bath　tooth　thank
much　chick　with
chip　teach　thick

Write the words that end like 🍎.

_____ _____ _____

Write the words that begin like 🪑.

_____ _____ _____

Write the words that end like 😀.

_____ _____ _____

Write the words that begin like 👉🖐.

_____ _____ _____

Write each group of words in alphabetical order.

much
each
teach
chore

1. _____
2. _____
3. _____
4. _____

tooth
bath
thank
with

1. _____
2. _____
3. _____
4. _____

Challenge! Write these words in alphabetical order.

thick
chip
think
chick

1. _____
2. _____
3. _____
4. _____

Looking Good

Word List

full	wool
stood	hook
bush	brook
book	push
pull	took
good	shook

Write the words with **u** that make the sound you hear in the middle of 🦶.

_____   _____

_____   _____

Write the words with double **o** that make the sound you hear in the middle of 🦶.

_____   _____

_____   _____

_____   _____

Write the words that begin like 🎈.

_____   _____

Which two words are opposites?

_____   _____

Circle the Word List words in the puzzle. Look across and down.

s	h	o	o	k	w	o	o	l	r
t	h	o	o	k	o	u	b	t	p
o	u	f	u	l	l	o	r	u	u
o	l	o	b	u	s	h	o	u	s
k	p	u	l	l	u	p	o	o	h
b	r	o	o	k	s	t	o	o	d

Write the words you circled in the puzzle.

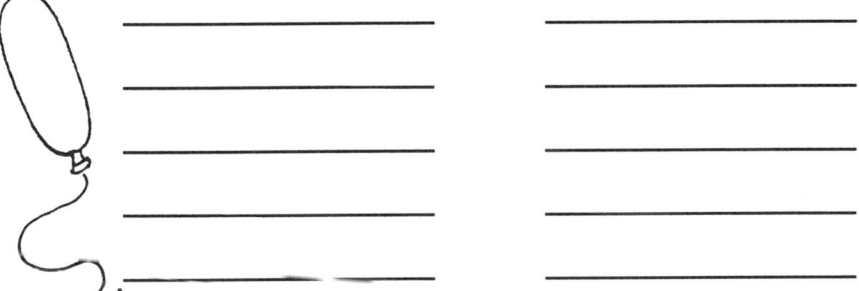

Which two words were not in the puzzle?

_____ _____

Challenge! Write one sentence using the two words you did not find in the puzzle.

_____

_____

Write the title of a good book you have read. Be sure to use capital letters where they belong.

_____

Showering Clouds

Word List

out   now   howl
clown   sound   ouch   owl
found   house   down   loud   town

Write the words with **ou** that sound like 🐭 .

_____ _____ _____ _____

_____ _____ _____ _____

Write the words with **ow** that sound like 👑 .

_____ _____ _____ _____

_____ _____ _____ _____

Write the word(s) that…
rhyme with 👑 . _____ _____ _____
begin with
a vowel. _____ _____ _____
end like 🐌 . _____ _____
begins like ✂ . _____
rhymes with ☁ . _____
rhyme with ground. _____ _____

Answer Key

Spelling Homework Booklet Grade 2

Bale Them Up

Word List: bait, sate, trail, pay, mail, way, plate, rake, age, day, pain, hay

Write the **ai** words that make the /ā/ sound.
bait, mail, trail, pain

Write the **ay** words that make the /ā/ sound.
pay, day, way, hay

Write the words ending with **e** that make the /ā/ sound.
safe, plate, rake, age

Write the letters that make the /ā/ sound.
ai, ay, a-e

---

1. Please put the **plate** on the table.
2. Which **way** do we go now?
3. Robin likes to **rake** the leaves.
4. Todd put the coins in the **safe**.
5. He could read by the **age** of six.
6. Ben put the **bait** on the hook.
7. The horses will eat the **hay**.
8. They will **pay** a dime for the pony ride.
9. We like to hike the **trail** to the lake.
10. It is a sunny **day**.
11. Did I get a letter in the **mail**?
12. He felt a lot of **pain** when he stepped on the nail.

Keep the Beat

Word List: mean, feet, deep, meal, team, keep, each, sweet, tree, treat, sneeze, leave

Write the double **e** words that make the /ē/ sound.
feet, sweet, deep, tree, keep, sneeze

Write the **ea** words that make the /ē/ sound.
mean, each, meal, treat, team, leave

Write the letters that make the /ē/ sound.
ee, ea

---

1. We must **leave** for school now.
2. The cake tastes very **sweet**.
3. The water in the lake is very **deep**.
4. There is a balloon for **each** of us.
5. What can we eat for our **meal**?
6. The **mean** dog barked at me.
7. After walking all the way home, his **feet** were sore.
8. Rob is glad that he will be on Jeff's baseball **team**.
9. When you have a cold, you sometimes **sneeze** a lot.
10. Please **keep** your desk neat.
11. The bird built a nest on a branch of the oak **tree**.
12. Ice cream is Irene's favorite **treat**.

A Mine Find

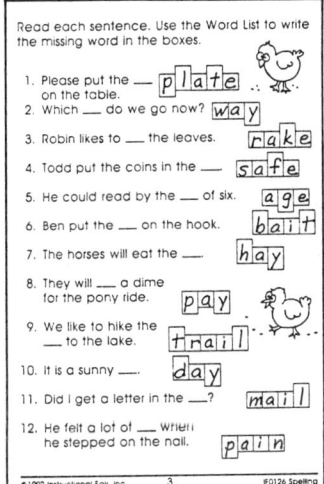

Word List: night, dry, find, stripe, wide, fly, smile, light, kind, cry, high, mind

Write the words ending with **e** that make the /ī/ sound.
stripe, wide, smile

Write the **igh** words that make the /ī/ sound.
night, light, high

Write the words ending with **y** that make the /ī/ sound.
dry, fly, cry

Write the words with **i** followed by **nd** that make the /ī/ sound.
find, kind, mind

Read each clue. Write the correct word from the maze on each line. Then trace a path from the miner to his find in the same order as your answers.

1. Opposite of wet — dry
2. Opposite of laugh — cry
3. Opposite of mean — kind
4. To obey your parents — mind
5. Opposite of day — night
6. You do this when you are happy — smile
7. Opposite of narrow — wide
8. You need this to see in the dark — light
9. What a bird does — fly
10. Not low, but... — high
11. A band of color — stripe
12. To discover — find

Coasting Along

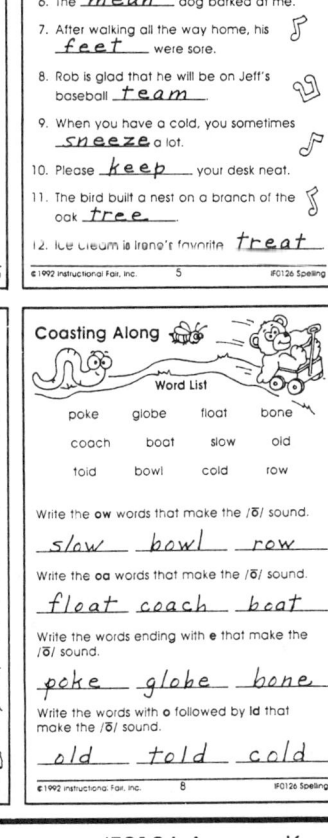

Word List: poke, globe, float, bone, coach, boat, slow, old, told, bowl, cold, row

Write the **ow** words that make the /ō/ sound.
slow, bowl, row

Write the **oa** words that make the /ō/ sound.
float, coach, boat

Write the words ending with **e** that make the /ō/ sound.
poke, globe, bone

Write the words with **o** followed by **ld** that make the /ō/ sound.
old, told, cold

©1992 Instructional Fair, Inc. IF0126 Answer Key

Read each sentence. Use the Word List to write the missing word in the boxes.

1. We have a new ___ for our football team. **coach**
2. Mother ___ me to mow the grass. **told**
3. Please put the oranges in a ___. **bowl**
4. You can find the United States on a ___. **globe**
5. Jody gave her dog a ___. **bone**
6. It was so ___, the water froze. **cold**
7. My ___ coat has a hole in it. **old**
8. Don't ___ your finger with the pin. **poke**
9. They will row the ___ across the lake. **boat** 
10. There was so much traffic that we had to ___ down. **slow**
11. Put all of the chairs in one ___. **row**
12. Will the raft ___ or sink? **float**

Parachuting

Word List: tube, zoo, balloon, moon, boot, moose, food, tune, cool, rude, room, pool

Write the words ending with e that make the /ū/ sound.
tube   tune   rude

Write the double o words that make the /ū/ sound.
zoo   boot   cool
balloon   moose   room
moon   food   pool

Write the words that rhyme with these pictures.
balloon   moon   tune
cool   pool   ✗
food   rude

Read each clue. Use the Word List to write the words on the lines. Then use the numbered letters to solve the code.

1. A kind of flying toy — **balloon**
2. You can sing it. — **tune**
3. Opposite of warm — **cool**
4. Like a hose or straw — **tube**
5. A part of a house — **room**
6. A kind of shoe — **boot**
7. An animal with antlers — **moose**
8. It shines at night. — **moon**
9. You can swim in it. — **pool**
10. Impolite — **rude**
11. What you eat — **food**
12. Where some animals live — **zoo**

Super cool fun!

Now Docking

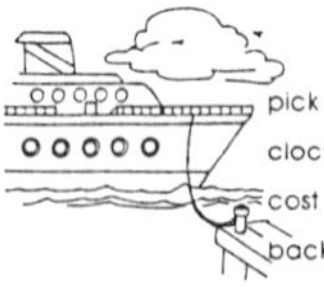

Word List: pick, cap, lock, clock, kick, pack, cost, flock, king, back, snack, sick

Write the words ending with ck that make the /k/ sound.
pick   kick   back
lock   pack   snack
clock   flock   sick

Write the words beginning with c that make the /k/ sound.
cap   clock   cost

Write the words beginning with k that make the /k/ sound.
kick   king

Write the words ending with ck and beginning with c or k that make the /k/ sound.
clock   kick

Write the words that rhyme with 🐤
pick   kick   sick

Write the words that rhyme with ☁
lock   clock   flock

Write the words that rhyme with 📦
pack   back   snack

Read each clue. Use the Word List to write the correct word on the line. Then circle the words in the puzzle.

1. A kind of hat — **cap**
2. The price — **cost**
3. The ruler of a country — **king**
4. A group of geese — **flock**

c	o	s	t	t	k
l	l	o	c	k	n
o	s	p	i	a	g
c	k	a	k	p	c

Don't Be Stumped

Word List: desk, best, task, fast, stand, state, lost, ask, mask, stump, step, last

Write the words that begin like ⭐
stand   stump
state   step

Write the words that end with the same sounds as 🖥
desk   ask
task   mask

Write the words that end with the same sounds as 🐢
best   lost
fast   last

Read each sentence. Use the Word List to write the missing word.
1. Beth **lost** her new coat.
2. The chipmunk sat on the tree **stump**.
3. Dan wore a pirate **mask** to the costume party.
4. Put your book on the **desk**.
5. Watch your **step** when you get off the bus.
6. She lives in the **state** of New York.
7. Steve can run very **fast**.
8. They were the **last** ones to leave the house.
9. If you **stand** by the window, you can see the lightning.
10. Grandmother bakes the very **best** apple pie.
11. Stan must do a small **task** before he can play.
12. Did you **ask** your cousin to go to the game?

Camping Out

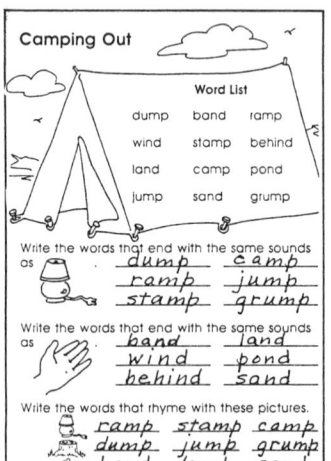

Word List: dump, band, ramp, wind, stamp, behind, land, camp, pond, jump, sand, grump

Write the words that end with the same sounds as 🏮
dump   camp
ramp   jump
stamp   grump

Write the words that end with the same sounds as ✋
band   land
wind   pond
behind   sand

Write the words that rhyme with these pictures.
ramp   stamp   camp
dump   jump   grump
band   land   sand

Make sure you have everything for the perfect camping trip. Write the Word List words in alphabetical order.

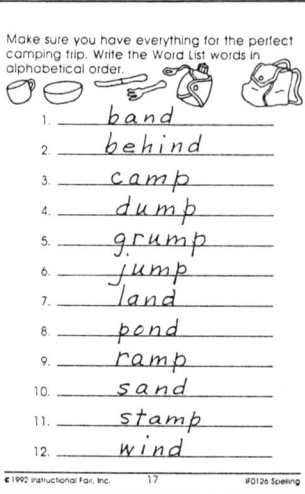

1. band
2. behind
3. camp
4. dump
5. grump
6. jump
7. land
8. pond
9. ramp
10. sand
11. stamp
12. wind

©1992 Instructional Fair, Inc.   IF0126 Answer Key

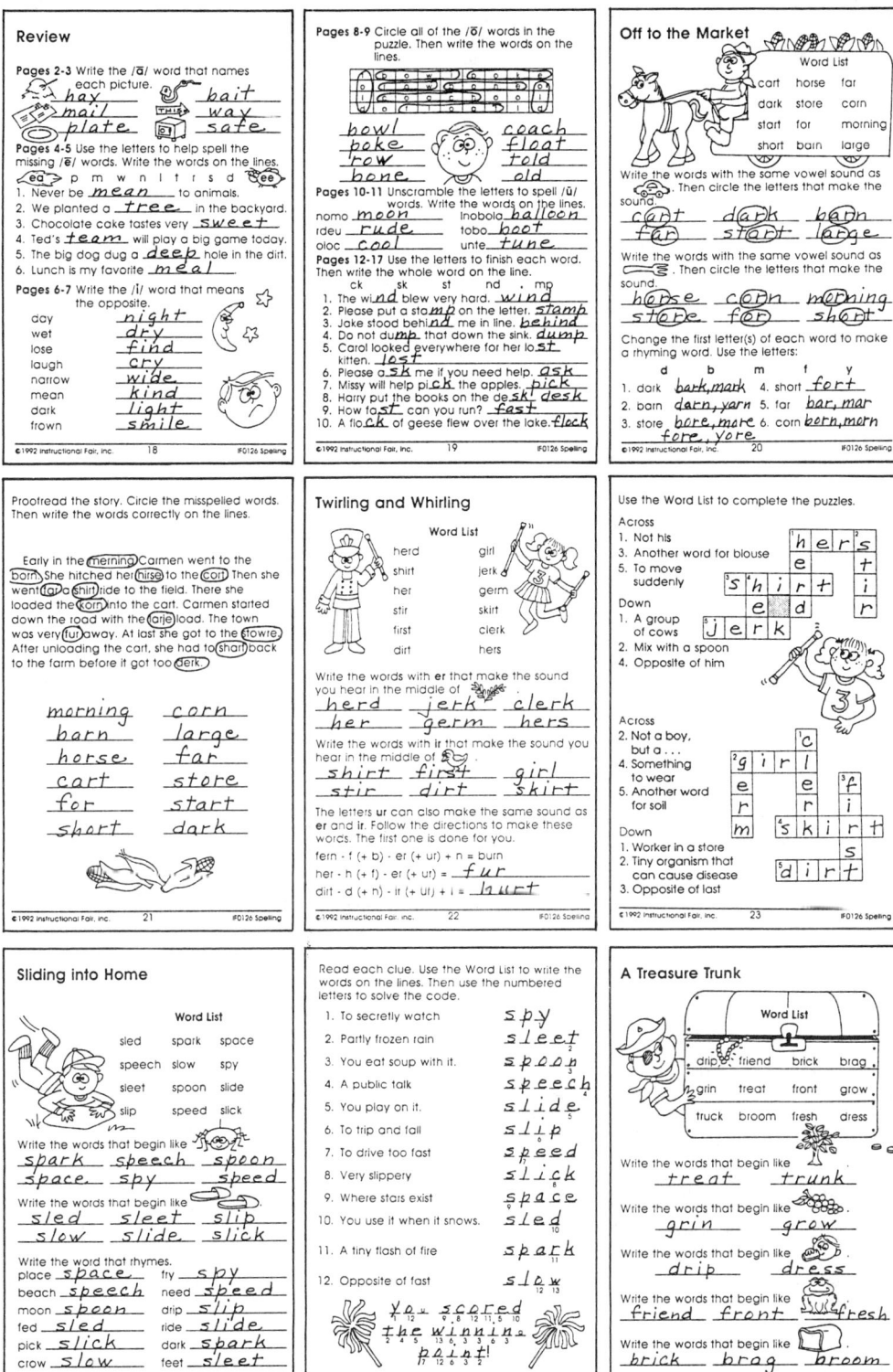

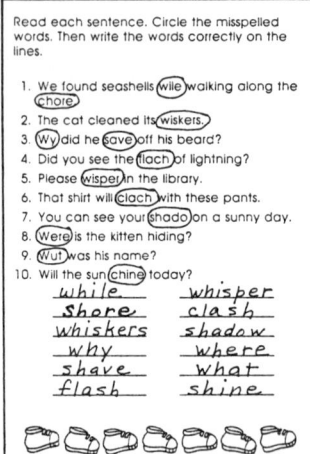

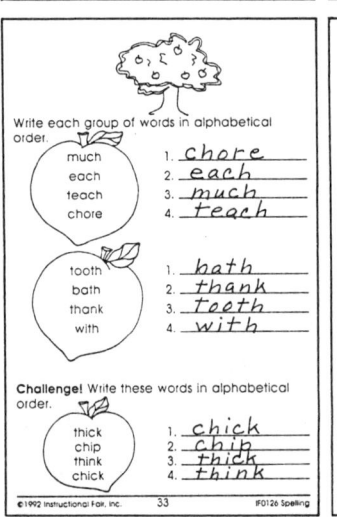

©1992 Instructional Fair, Inc. IF0126 Answer Key

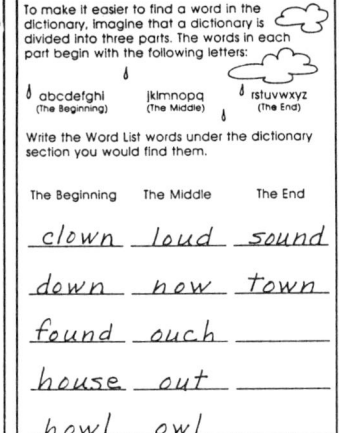
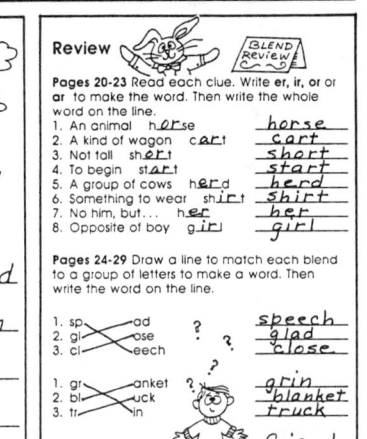
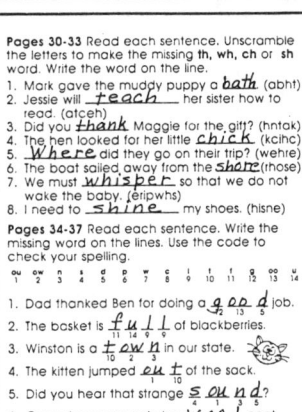
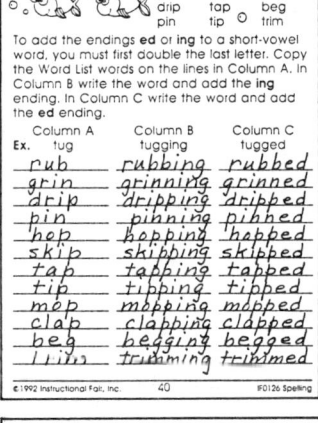
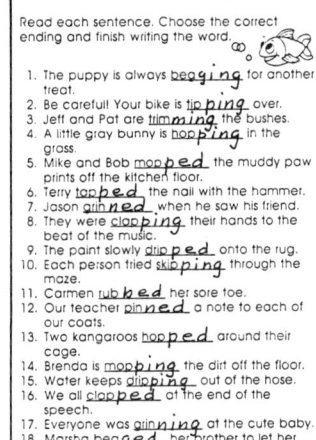

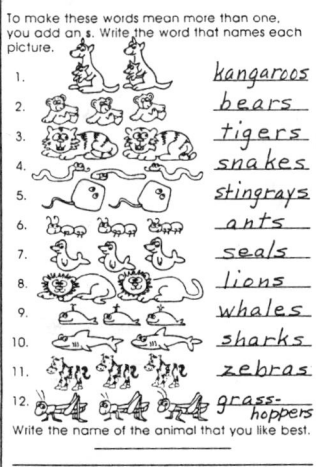
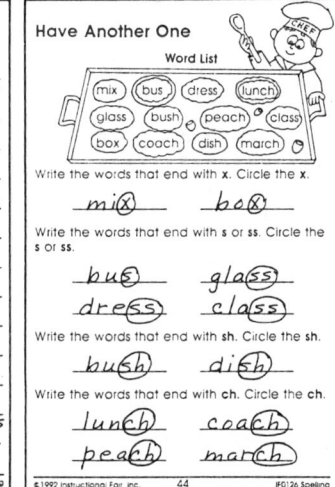

©1992 Instructional Fair, Inc.   IF0126 Answer Key

When a word ends with the letters **s, ss, x, ch** or **sh**, add the letters **es** to make the word mean more than one. Write each word from the Word List to make it mean more than one.

1.	mixes	7.	peaches
2.	buses	8.	classes
3.	dresses	9.	boxes
4.	lunches	10.	coaches
5.	glasses	11.	dishes
6.	bushes	12.	marches

Read each sentence. Use the Word List to write the correct word on the line.

1. Martha needs two mixes to make the cakes.
2. The puppies are hiding under these bushes.
3. Bill and Betty picked some peaches.
4. We ate our lunches in the park.
5. We filled three boxes with empty cans.
6. All three classes went on a field trip.
7. My sister bought two new dresses for school.
8. Long ago people traveled in coaches.
9. We filled all of the glasses with milk.
10. We helped grandmother wash the dishes.
11. The band played four marches during the parade.
12. We had to ride two buses to get to the zoo.

A Magical Compound

lunch girl note side cat some
house father man friend in book
fire box bed room fish thing
dog grand box ball sand foot

Write the two words that make up each compound word.

Word List		
1. lunchbox	lunch	box
2. notebook	note	book
3. fireman	fire	man
4. doghouse	dog	house
5. bedroom	bed	room
6. something	some	thing
7. catfish	cat	fish
8. football	foot	ball
9. inside	in	side
10. sandbox	sand	box
11. grandfather	grand	father
12. girlfriend	girl	friend

Read each clue. Use the words in the magician's hat to write each word. Then write the compound word.

Clue	Words	Compound word
1. A barking animal / A place to live	dog / house	doghouse
2. Where you sleep / Part of a house	bed / room	bedroom
3. Opposite of boy / Opposite of enemy	girl / friend	girlfriend
4. Great or wonderful / Opposite of mother	grand / father	grandfather
5. A short letter / You read it.	note / book	notebook
6. Part of a leg / A toy	foot / ball	football
7. Opposite of out / Rhymes with ride	in / side	inside
8. It covers a beach. / You put things in it.	sand / box	sandbox
9. Meal at noontime / Rhymes with fox	lunch / box	lunchbox
10. A few / Rhymes with king	some / thing	something
11. An animal / An animal with fins	cat / fish	catfish
12. Flames / Opposite of woman	fire / man	fireman

Composing Compounds

Draw a line to match the two words that go together to make a compound word.

1. boy — friend
2. sail — boat
3. blue — bird
4. week — end
5. barn — yard
6. in — to
7. down — town
8. rain — coat
9. grand — mother
10. every — where
11. mail — box
12. back — pack

Write the compound words on the lines.

1.	boyfriend	7.	downtown
2.	sailboat	8.	raincoat
3.	bluebird	9.	grandmother
4.	weekend	10.	everywhere
5.	barnyard	11.	mailbox
6.	into	12.	backpack

Read each clue. Write the compound words from page 48 on the lines. Then use the numbered letters to solve the code.

1. A boy that is a friend — boyfriend
2. The end of a week — weekend
3. A part of town — downtown
4. To go inside of — into
5. A bag worn when hiking — backpack
6. A place on a farm — barnyard
7. Coat you wear in the rain — raincoat
8. In every place — everywhere
9. A boat with sails — sailboat
10. Special box for letters — mailbox
11. A bird with blue feathers — bluebird
12. Your mother or father's mother — grandmother

You wrote a masterpiece!

Write It Right!

Word List

deer, eye, plant, one, meat, won, dear, I, plain, eight, meet, ate

Read each word. Then write the two words that rhyme with it.

1. try	I	eye
2. seat	meet	meat
3. cane	plain	plane
4. sun	won	one
5. late	ate	eight
6. near	dear	deer

Write the word that names the picture. Then next to it write the word that sounds the same.

plane	plain
meat	meet
eye	I
one	won
deer	dear
eight	ate

Read each sentence. Use the Word List to write the missing word.

1. There are eight children on the bus.
2. Our family will fly to New York on a plane.
3. Fred will meet us on the playground.
4. Do you like chocolate-covered or plain donuts?
5. A deer is a beautiful forest animal.
6. Our class won the prize for reading the most books.
7. My friend and I like to plant flowers.
8. We ate our lunches in the park.
9. The blowing dust got in his eye.
10. My grandmother is a very dear person.
11. May I please have one more cookie?
12. What kind of meat do you like to eat?

Pick a Pair of Pears

Word List

road, write, see, hear, for, our, four, here, right, sea, rode, hour

Read each clue. Write the correct word on the line.

1. Three plus one — four
2. Fish live here — sea
3. A street — road
4. Your eyes do this. — see
5. Opposite of left — right
6. This is ___ you. — for
7. Your ears do this. — hear
8. Opposite of there — here
9. Belonging to us — our
10. Did ride — rode
11. Use a pencil to do this. — write
12. A clock tells you this. — hour

Write each pair of words that sound alike. Remember, they do not mean the same and are not spelled the same.

road - rode	see - sea
write - right	for - four
hear - here	our - hour

Circle the Word List words in the puzzle. Look across and down.

y	o	o	u	r	s	s	e	e	h
r	i	g	h	t	l	e	h	t	e
f	t	f	o	u	r	o	o	s	r
o	w	r	i	t	e	i	u	e	e
r	t	h	e	a	r	r	r	a	h

Write the words you circled in the puzzzle.

our	hear
see	hour
right	sea
four	here
write	for

Which two words were not in the puzzle?

rode road

Challenge! Write one sentence using the two words you did not find in the puzzle.

Answers will vary.

©1992 Instructional Fair, Inc.

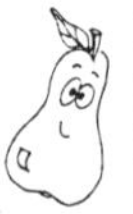

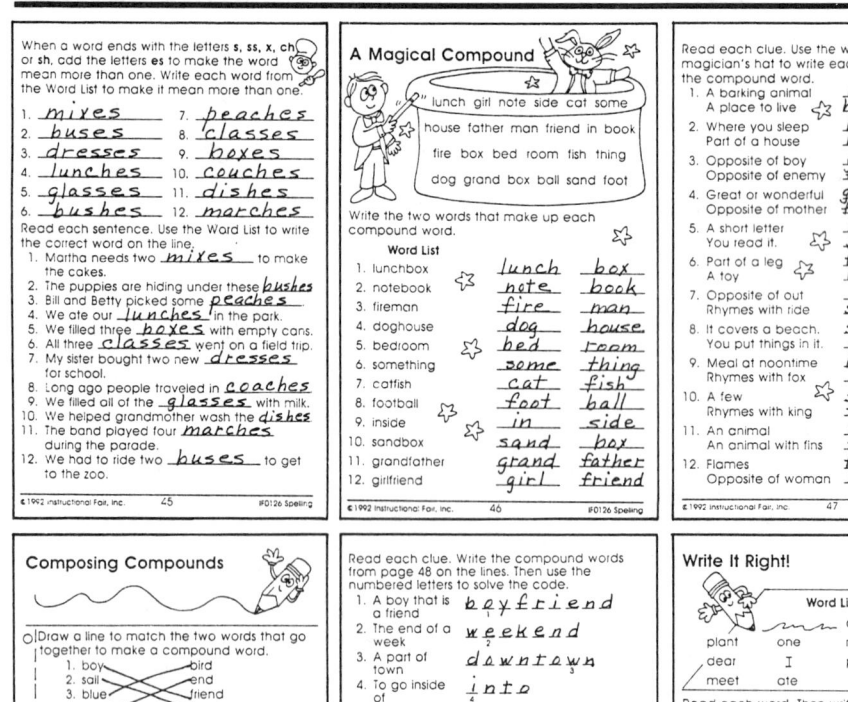

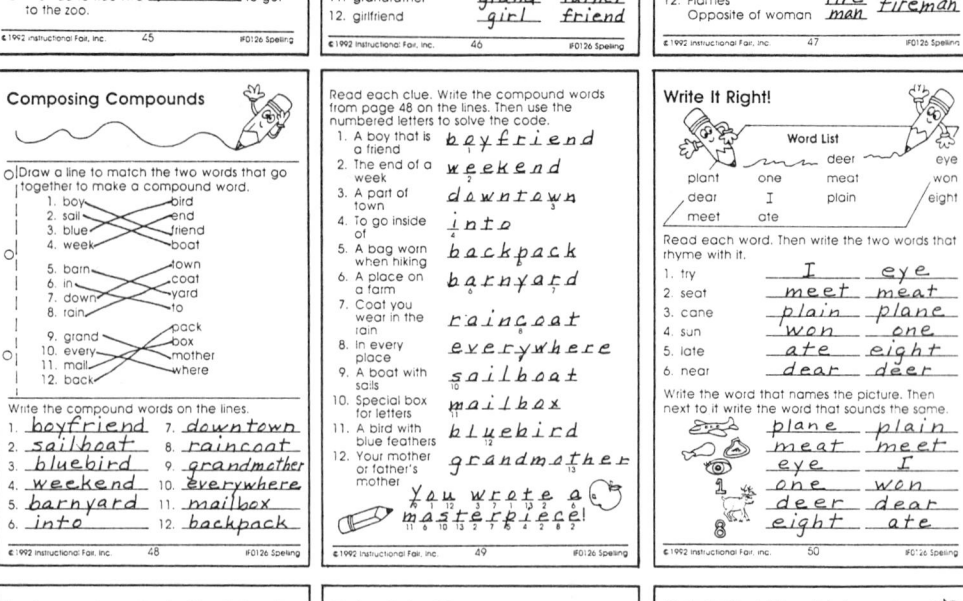

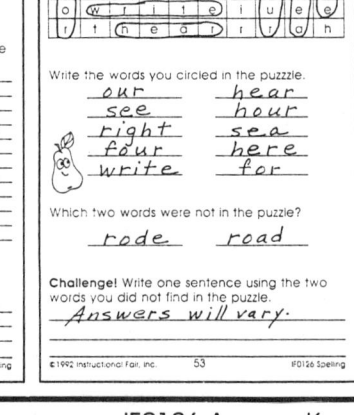

Review

Pages 40-41 Read each sentence. Add ing or ed to the word and write it on the line.
1. Everyone **clapped** when Mike got the award. (clap)
2. The rain is **dripping** off the roof. (drip)
3. A woodpecker is **tapping** on the tree bark. (tap)
4. We **mopped** the sticky jam off the floor. (mop)
5. Mom is busy **trimming** my sister's hair. (trim)
6. Pat **rubbed** his sore elbow. (rub)
7. Two kangaroos are **hopping** in the tall grass. (hop)
8. The clerk **pinned** the tags on the dresses. (pin)

Pages 42-45 Read each word. Then write the word and add s or es to make it mean more than one.

seal	**seals**	bush	**bushes**
bus	**buses**	shark	**sharks**
stingray	**stingrays**	coach	**coaches**
lunch	**lunches**	lion	**lions**
zebra	**zebras**	glass	**glasses**
box	**boxes**	tiger	**tigers**

Pages 46-49 Draw a line to match the two words that go together to make a compound word. Then write the word on the line.
1. week — mother — **weekend**
2. mail — end — **mailbox**
3. back — box — **backpack**
4. grand — thing — **grandmother**
5. some — pack — **something**
6. down — book — **downtown**
7. note — room — **notebook**
8. bed — town — **bedroom**

Pages 50-53 Write the correct word on the line.

meet - meat	I - eye
road - rode	for - four
our - hour	write - right
	hear - here	see - sea

1. Do you **hear** someone knocking at the door?
2. Mike and **I** are going to be in a play.
3. A ranger can **see** far from the lookout.
4. We must put on **our** coats before going outside.
5. Pete **rode** his bike to the park.
6. I will sharpen my pencil before I **write** the letter.
7. We will **meet** grandmother at the station.
8. Vern planted **four** apple trees in the yard.

Dont' Be Confused

Word List
would, away, guess
many, love, trouble
nice, every, nothing
any, party, goes

Use the Word List to unscramble the letters to spell a word. Write the word on the line.

1. o h i n n t g — **nothing**
2. l t e u o r b — **trouble**
3. s u s g e — **guess**
4. a y a w — **away**
5. o g s e — **goes**
6. i e c n — **nice**
7. a y m n — **many**
8. e l v o — **love**
9. u w d l o — **would**
10. e e y v r — **every**
11. r p y t a — **party**
12. y n a — **any**

Write the three words above that you think are the hardest to spell. **Answers will vary.**

Use the Word List to complete the puzzle.

Across
2. One or some
3. A celebration
7. Opposite of everything
9. All
11. Opposite of hate
12. Opposite of comes

Down
1. Several
4. Difficulty
5. Courteous and polite
6. Rhymes with say
8. Rhymes with mess
10. Homonym of wood

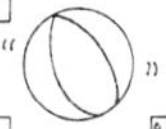

Crossword answers: many, party, nothing, every, love, goes, would

---

A Family Gathering

Write the word that names the person(s) in each picture.
1. **baby**
2. **brother**
3. **father**
4. **twins**
5. **grandfather**
6. **aunt**
7. **boy**
8. **grandmother**
9. **sister**
10. **uncle**
11. **mother**
12. **girl**

Read each clue. Write the correct words from page 58 on the lines. Then use the numbered letters to solve the code.

1. Another word for mom — **mother**
2. Dad's mother — **grandmother**
3. Mom's father — **grandfather**
4. Mom's sister — **aunt**
5. Dad's brother — **uncle**
6. Two persons from the same family born on the same day — **twins**
7. Opposite of girl — **boy**
8. A very small child — **baby**
9. Opposite of sister — **brother**
10. Another word for dad — **father**
11. Opposite of boy — **girl**
12. Opposite of brother — **sister**

Families are wonderful!

A Circus of Colors

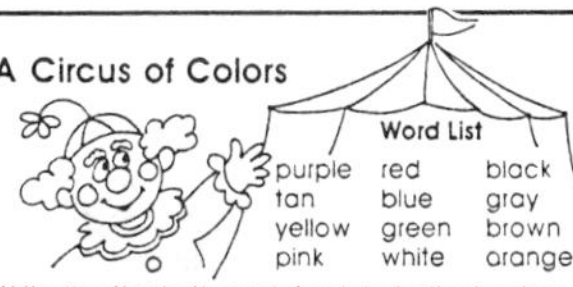

Word List
purple, red, black
tan, blue, gray
yellow, green, brown
pink, white, orange

Write the "color" words in alphabetical order.
1. **black**
2. **blue**
3. **brown**
4. **gray**
5. **green**
6. **orange**
7. **pink**
8. **purple**
9. **red**
10. **tan**
11. **white**
12. **yellow**

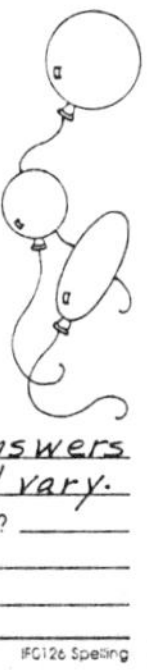

Which color do you like most? **Answers**
Which color do you like least? **will vary.**
What color is your favorite ice cream?
What color is your favorite fruit?
What color is your favorite chair?

Use the code to color the picture.
1—pink
2—yellow
3—black
4—white
5—purple
6—tan
7—blue
8—red
9—gray
10—orange
11—brown
12—green

Use the picture to write the missing color words on the lines.

Herman and Clyde are clowns. Herman is the tall clown with **tan** hair. Clyde is the short clown with **orange** hair. Both of them have **pink** noses. Herman always wears his old **brown** shirt and **red** socks. He has to use **white** suspenders to hold up his big **green** pants. Clyde looks funny in his **blue** and **yellow** polka-dotted costume. He says that his **purple** hat is lucky. Clyde's feet are not as big as his **black** shoes. Would you like to have a **gray** elephant balloon, too?

The Countdown Begins

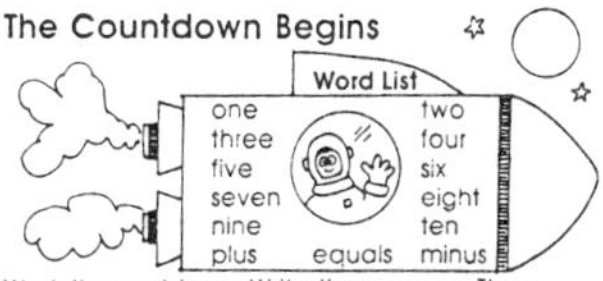

Word List
one, two, three, four, five, six, seven, eight, nine, ten, plus, equals, minus

Work the problems. Write the answers. Then write the answers using the correct number words.

1. 18 − 9 = **9** — **nine**
2. 12 − 8 = **4** — **four**
3. 14 − 7 = **7** — **seven**
4. 10 − 9 = **1** — **one**
5. 12 − 7 = **5** — **five**
6. 13 − 3 = **10** — **ten**
7. 11 − 5 = **6** — **six**
8. 12 − 9 = **3** — **three**
9. 13 − 5 = **8** — **eight**
10. 10 − 8 = **2** — **two**

Write the math problems using only words.
4 + 6 = 10 — **four plus six equals ten**
8 − 3 = 5 — **eight minus three equals five**
9 − 7 = 2 — **nine minus seven equals two**
1 + 5 = 6 — **one plus five equals six**

©1992 Instructional Fair, Inc.   IF0126 Answer Key

This graph tells how many stars each person saw last night. Use the graph to answer the questions. Write the correct number word on the line.

Name Number of Stars

Mandy									
Beth									
Ray									
Matt									
Darlene									
Sam									
Andrea									
Pete									
Carl									
Greta									

How many more stars did...
1. Mandy see than Beth? **six**
2. Carl see than Greta? **two**
3. Pete see than Ray? **one**
4. Sam see than Darlene? **five**
5. Matt see than Greta? **three**

How many stars did these people see altogether?
1. Pete and Beth **seven**
2. Greta and Andrea **ten**
3. Andrea and Darlene **four**
4. Pete and Ray **nine**
5. Beth and Sam **eight**

Write the word for each symbol.
= **equals**
+ **plus**
− **minus**

Cool Choices

(first) chocolate (second) vanilla (third) strawberry (fourth) lemon
(fifth) lime (sixth) cherry (seventh) rockyroad (eighth) peach
(ninth) blueberry (tenth) butternut (eleventh) orange (twelfth) pineapple

Read the name of each ice-cream flavor. Write the word from above that tells which choice it is.

1. cherry — **sixth**
2. lemon — **fourth**
3. vanilla — **second**
4. orange — **eleventh**
5. blueberry — **ninth**
6. strawberry — **third**
7. rockyroad — **seventh**
8. chocolate — **first**
9. lime — **fifth**
10. butternut — **tenth**
11. pineapple — **twelfth**
12. peach — **eighth**

You decide! Write the ordinal number word to tell in what order you would choose each flavor.

1. blueberry
2. butternut
3. cherry
4. chocolate
5. lemon
6. lime
7. orange
8. peach
9. vanilla
10. rockyroad
11. strawberry
12. pineapple

Answers will vary.

Write the ordinal number word under each picture.

first   second   third

What a Busy Day

Word List: Friday, week, Tuesday, Wednesday, Sunday, days, Saturday, yesterday, Monday, Thursday, tomorrow, today

Write the days of the week in the correct order.
1. Sunday
2. Monday
3. Tuesday
4. Wednesday
5. Thursday
6. Friday
7. Saturday

Read each clue. Write the correct word on the line.
1. The day before today — **yesterday**
2. This day — **today**
3. Seven days make this. — **week**
4. The day after today — **tomorrow**
5. A week has seven of them. — **days**

Read the calendar. The days of the week are written in abbreviated form.

Sun.	Mon.	Tues.	Wed.	Thurs.	Fri.	Sat.
Visit Uncle Joe	Go to the bookstore	Go fishing	Baseball game	Skateboard contest	Help Mom clean house	Go to the beach

Use the calendar to write the missing word on the line. Write the whole word for each day of the week.
1. We will go fishing on **Tuesday**.
2. On **Saturday** we will be able to look for seashells.
3. We can buy two new books on **Monday**.
4. We will have fun at Uncle Joe's farm on **Sunday**.
5. I hope our team wins the game on **Wednesday**.
6. **Friday** morning we will be busy helping mom.
7. Dad's buying us new skateboards for the contest this **Thursday**.
8. The calendar shows one whole **week**.
9. If today is Friday, then **tomorrow** is Saturday.
10. The calendar shows all seven **days** of a week.
11. If today is Tuesday, then **yesterday** was Monday.
12. If yesterday was Monday, then **today** is Tuesday.

'Tis the Season for Holidays

Word List: Valentine's Day, Easter, Halloween, summer, Christmas, fall, Fourth of July, St. Patrick's Day, New Year's Day, Thanksgiving, winter, spring

Read each clue. Write the correct holiday or season on the line. Remember to capitalize the first letter of a holiday.

1. You put on a costume. — **Halloween**
2. First day of the year — **New Year's Day**
3. Wear something green. — **St. Patrick's**
4. Fireworks in the sky — **Fourth of July**
5. Time for presents — **Christmas**
6. Hearts everywhere — **Valentine's Day**
7. Look for hidden eggs. — **Easter**
8. Give thanks. — **Thanksgiving**
9. Cold and snowy — **winter**
10. Leaves change color. — **fall**
11. Sunny and hot — **summer**
12. Flowers bloom. — **spring**

Write a sentence about your favorite holiday.
Answers will vary.

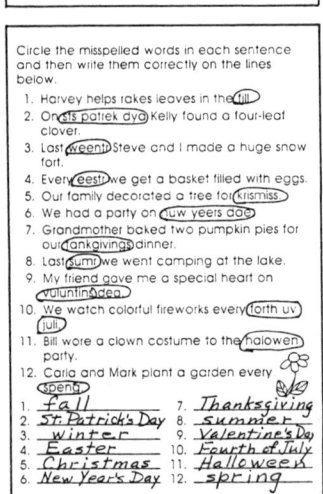

Circle the misspelled words in each sentence and then write them correctly on the lines below.

1. Harvey helps rakes leaves in the (fill).
2. On (sts patrek dy) Kelly found a four-leaf clover.
3. Last (weenti) Steve and I made a huge snow fort.
4. Every (eesti) we get a basket filled with eggs.
5. Our family decorated a tree for (krismiss).
6. We had a party on (luw yeers da).
7. Grandmother baked two pumpkin pies for our (tanksgiving) dinner.
8. Last (sumr) we went camping at the lake.
9. My friend gave me a special heart on (voluntinodea).
10. We watch colorful fireworks every (forth uv) (juli).
11. Bill wore a clown costume to the (haloween) party.
12. Carla and Mark plant a garden every (spreng).

1. fall
2. St. Patrick's Day
3. winter
4. Easter
5. Christmas
6. New Year's Day
7. Thanksgiving
8. summer
9. Valentine's Day
10. Fourth of July
11. Halloween
12. spring

Review

Pages 56-57 Circle the correctly spelled missing word for each sentence.
1. Everyone had fun at the Halloween parde / (party).
2. _____ you like to pet a giraffe? (Would) / Wood
3. What is the _____ with that computer? (trouble) / trubel
4. Can you _____ how many apples are in the basket? gess / (guess)

Pages 58-59 Unscramble the letters to spell words that name people in a family. Write the words on the lines.
roebrth — **brother**
ncleu — **uncle**
unat — **aunt**
ahfetr — **father**
abyb — **baby**
othmre — **mother**
rdganohter — **grandfather**
gndrmaoethr — **grandmother**
irsste — **sister**
wntis — **twins**

Pages 60-61 Write the best color words for each item.
ripe tomato — **red**
banana — **yellow**
elephant — **gray**
twigs — **brown**
zebra — **black**
grape jam — **purple**
sky — **blue**
pumpkin — **orange**
plants — **green**
and — **white**

Pages 62-63 Work the problems. Circle the correct answer, and then write the correct number word.

1. $17 - 8 =$ (9) or 8 — **nine**
2. $12 - 9 =$ 6 or (3) — **three**
3. $15 - 9 =$ 5 or (6) — **six**
4. $11 - 9 =$ (2) or 3 — **two**
5. $13 - 8 =$ (5) or 4 — **five**

Pages 64-65 Write the correct ordinal number words.
1st — **first**   7th — **seventh**
2nd — **second**   8th — **eighth**
3rd — **third**   9th — **ninth**

Pages 66-67 Write the days of the week in alphabetical order.
1. Friday
2. Monday
3. Saturday
4. Sunday
5. Thursday
6. Tuesday
7. Wednesday

Pages 68-69 Write the name of each holiday or season.
Valentine's Day, St. Patrick's Day, Christmas, Easter, Halloween, winter, summer, Thanksgiving

© 1992 Instructional Fair, Inc.   IF0126 Answer Key

/ou/

To make it easier to find a word in the dictionary, imagine that a dictionary is divided into three parts. The words in each part begin with the following letters:

abcdefghi jklmnopq rstuvwxyz
(The Beginning) (The Middle) (The End)

Write the Word List words under the dictionary section you would find them.

The Beginning	The Middle	The End
_____	_____	_____
_____	_____	_____
_____	_____	_____
_____	_____	_____
_____	_____	_____

Review

pages 20-37

Pages 20-23 Read each clue. Write **er, ir, or** or **ar** to make the word. Then write the whole word on the line.

1. An animal   h___se   _____
2. A kind of wagon   c___t   _____
3. Not tall   sh___t   _____
4. To begin   st___t   _____
5. A group of cows   h___d   _____
6. Something to wear   sh___t   _____
7. No him, but...   h___   _____
8. Opposite of boy   g___l   _____

Pages 24-29 Draw a line to match each blend to a group of letters to make a word. Then write the word on the line.

1. sp   ad   _____
2. gl   ose   _____
3. cl   eech   _____

1. gr   anket   _____
2. bl   uck   _____
3. tr   in   _____

1. fr   oom   _____
2. dr   ess   _____
3. br   iend   _____

Pages 30-33 Read each sentence. Unscramble the letters to make the missing **th, wh, ch** or **sh** word. Write the word on the line.

1. Mark gave the muddy puppy a _____. (abht)
2. Jessie will _____ her sister how to read. (atceh)
3. Did you _____ Maggie for the gift? (hntak)
4. The hen looked for her little _____. (kcihc)
5. _____ did they go on their trip? (wehre)
6. The boat sailed away from the _____. (rhose)
7. We must _____ so that we do not wake the baby. (eripwhs)
8. I need to _____ my shoes. (hisne)

Pages 34-37 Read each sentence. Write the missing word on the lines. Use the code to check your spelling.

ou	ow	n	s	d	p	w	c	l	t	f	g	oo	u
1	2	3	4	5	6	7	8	9	10	11	12	13	14

1. Dad thanked Ben for doing a __ __ __ job.
                                               12 13 5
2. The basket is __ __ __ __ of blackberries.
                       11 14 9 9
3. Winston is a __ __ __ in our state.
                   10 2 3
4. The kitten jumped __ __ of the sack.
                        1 10
5. Did you hear that strange __ __ __ __?
                               4 1 3 5
6. Casey keeps warm in her __ __ __ coat.
                               7 13 9
7. Percy is a very funny __ __ __ __.
                            8 9 2 3
8. Can Adam __ __ __ __ the wagon all the way home?
                 6 14 9 9

On the Double

Word List

rub	hop	mop
grin	skip	clap
drip	tap	beg
pin	tip	trim

To add the endings **ed** or **ing** to a short-vowel word, you must first double the last letter. Copy the Word List words on the lines in Column A. In Column B write the word and add the **ing** ending. In Column C write the word and add the **ed** ending.

	Column A	Column B	Column C
Ex.	tug	tugging	tugged

_____   _____   _____
_____   _____   _____
_____   _____   _____
_____   _____   _____
_____   _____   _____
_____   _____   _____
_____   _____   _____
_____   _____   _____
_____   _____   _____
_____   _____   _____
_____   _____   _____
_____   _____   _____

adding ed and ing

Read each sentence. Choose the correct ending and finish writing the word.

1. The puppy is always <u>beg_____</u> for another treat.
2. Be careful! Your bike is <u>tip_____</u> over.
3. Jeff and Pat are <u>trim_____</u> the bushes.
4. A little gray bunny is <u>hop_____</u> in the grass.
5. Mike and Bob <u>mop_____</u> the muddy paw prints off the kitchen floor.
6. Terry <u>tap_____</u> the nail with the hammer.
7. Jason <u>grin_____</u> when he saw his friend.
8. They were <u>clap_____</u> their hands to the beat of the music.
9. The paint slowly <u>drip_____</u> onto the rug.
10. Each person tried <u>skip_____</u> through the maze.
11. Carmen <u>rub_____</u> her sore toe.
12. Our teacher <u>pin_____</u> a note to each of our coats.
13. Two kangaroos <u>hop_____</u> around their cage.
14. Brenda is <u>mop_____</u> the dirt off the floor.
15. Water keeps <u>drip_____</u> out of the hose.
16. We all <u>clap_____</u> at the end of the speech.
17. Everyone was <u>grin_____</u> at the cute baby.
18. Marsha <u>beg_____</u> her brother to let her use his new mitt.

Awesome Animals

Word List

stingray
grasshopper
snake
lion
whale
tiger

seal
shark
bear
ant
zebra
kangaroo

Write the names of the animals in alphabetical order.

1. _____
2. _____
3. _____
4. _____
5. _____
6. _____
7. _____
8. _____
9. _____
10. _____
11. _____
12. _____

Write the names of the animals that you would find in a zoo.

_____   _____   _____

_____   _____   _____

Write the names of the animals that you might find in a public aquarium.

_____   _____

_____   _____

Write the names of two animals that are insects.

_____   _____

©1992 Instructional Fair, Inc.   IF0126 Spelling

"animal" words

To make these words mean more than one, you add an **s**. Write the word that names each picture.

1. _____
2. _____
3. _____
4. _____
5. _____
6. _____
7. _____
8. _____
9. _____
10. _____
11. _____
12. _____

Write the name of the animal that you like best.

_____

Have Another One

Word List

mix, bus, dress, lunch, glass, bush, peach, class, box, coach, dish, march

Write the words that end with **x**. Circle the **x**.

_____   _____

Write the words that end with **s** or **ss**. Circle the **s** or **ss**.

_____   _____

_____   _____

Write the words that end with **sh**. Circle the **sh**.

_____   _____

Write the words that end with **ch**. Circle the **ch**.

_____   _____

_____   _____

plurals

When a word ends with the letters **s, ss, x, ch** or **sh**, add the letters **es** to make the word mean more than one. Write each word from the Word List to make it mean more than one.

1. _____   7. _____
2. _____   8. _____
3. _____   9. _____
4. _____   10. _____
5. _____   11. _____
6. _____   12. _____

Read each sentence. Use the W_____ the correct word on the line.

1. Martha needs two _____ to make the cakes.
2. The puppies are hiding under these _____.
3. Bill and Betty picked some _____.
4. We ate our _____ in the park.
5. We filled three _____ with empty cans.
6. All three _____ went on a field trip.
7. My sister bought two new _____ for school.
8. Long ago people traveled in _____.
9. We filled all of the _____ with milk.
10. We helped grandmother wash the _____.
11. The band played four _____ during the parade.
12. We had to ride two _____ to get to the zoo.

A Magical Compound

lunch girl note side cat some
house father man friend in book
fire box bed room fish thing
dog grand box ball sand foot

Write the two words that make up each compound word.

Word List

1. lunchbox
2. notebook
3. fireman
4. doghouse
5. bedroom
6. something
7. catfish
8. football
9. inside
10. sandbox
11. grandfather
12. girlfriend

compounds

Read each clue. Use the words in the magician's hat to write each word. Then write the compound word.

1. A barking animal
   A place to live
2. Where you sleep
   Part of a house
3. Opposite of boy
   Opposite of enemy
4. Great or wonderful
   Opposite of mother
5. A short letter
   You read it.
6. Part of a leg
   A toy
7. Opposite of out
   Rhymes with ride
8. It covers a beach.
   You put things in it.
9. Meal at noontime
   Rhymes with fox
10. A few
    Rhymes with king
11. An animal
    An animal with fins
12. Flames
    Opposite of woman

Composing Compounds

Draw a line to match the two words that go together to make a compound word.

1.	boy	bird
2.	sail	end
3.	blue	friend
4.	week	boat
5.	barn	town
6.	in	coat
7.	down	yard
8.	rain	to
9.	grand	pack
10.	every	box
11.	mail	mother
12.	back	where

Write the compound words on the lines.

1. _____ 7. _____
2. _____ 8. _____
3. _____ 9. _____
4. _____ 10. _____
5. _____ 11. _____
6. _____ 12. _____

compounds

Read each clue. Write the compound words from page 48 on the lines. Then use the numbered letters to solve the code.

1. A boy that is a friend ‗ _ _ _ _ _ _ _
         1

2. The end of a week _ _ _ _ _ _ _
      2

3. A part of town _ _ _ _ _ _ _ _
               3

4. To go inside of _ _ _ _
    4

5. A bag worn when hiking _ _ _ _ _ _ _ _
        5

6. A place on a farm _ _ _ _ _ _ _ _
    6   7

7. Coat you wear in the rain _ _ _ _ _ _ _ _
       8

8. In every place _ _ _ _ _ _ _ _ _
        9

9. A boat with sails _ _ _ _ _ _ _ _
   10

10. Special box for letters _ _ _ _ _ _ _
    11

11. A bird with blue feathers _ _ _ _ _ _ _
       12

12. Your mother or father's mother _ _ _ _ _ _ _ _ _
              13

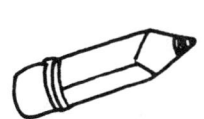 _ _ _ _ _ _ _ _ _ _ !
  9 1 12 3 7 1 13 2 6

_ _ _ _ _ _ _ _ _ _
11 6 10 13 2 7 5 4 2 8 2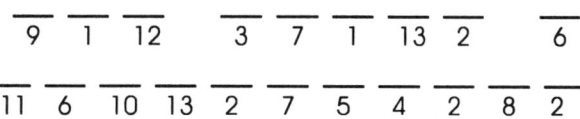

Write It Right!

Word List

plane	one	deer	eye
dear	I	meat	won
meet	ate	plain	eight

Read each word. Then write the two words that rhyme with it.

1. try _____ _____
2. seat _____ _____
3. cane _____ _____
4. sun _____ _____
5. late _____ _____
6. near _____ _____

Write the word that names the picture. Then next to it write the word that sounds the same.

_____ _____
_____ _____
_____ _____
_____ _____
_____ _____

homonyms

Read each sentence. Use the Word List to write the missing word.

1. There are _____ children on the bus.

2. Our family will fly to New York on a _____.

3. Fred will _____ us on the playground.

4. Do you like chocolate-covered or _____ donuts?

5. A _____ is a beautiful forest animal.

6. Our class _____ the prize for reading the most books.

7. My friend and _____ like to plant flowers.

8. We _____ our lunches in the park.

9. The blowing dust got in his _____.

10. My grandmother is a very _____ person.

11. May I please have _____ more cookie?

12. What kind of _____ do you like to eat?

Pick a Pair of Pears

Word List

road, write, see, hear, for, our, four, here, right, sea, rode, hour

Read each clue. Write the correct word on the line.

1. Three plus one _____
2. Fish live here _____
3. A street _____
4. Your eyes do this. _____
5. Opposite of left _____
6. This is ___ you. _____
7. Your ears do this. _____
8. Opposite of there _____
9. Belonging to us _____
10. Did ride _____
11. Use a pencil to do this. _____
12. A clock tells you this. _____

Write each pair of words that sound alike. Remember, they do not mean the same and are not spelled the same.

_____   _____
_____   _____
_____   _____

homonyms

Circle the Word List words in the puzzle.
Look across and down.

y	o	o	u	r	s	s	e	e	h
r	i	g	h	t	l	e	h	t	e
f	t	f	o	u	r	o	o	s	r
o	w	r	i	t	e	i	u	e	e
r	t	h	e	a	r	r	r	a	h

Write the words you circled in the puzzzle.

_____   _____

_____   _____

_____   _____

_____   _____

Which two words were not in the puzzle?

_____   _____

Challenge! Write one sentence using the two words you did not find in the puzzle.

_____

_____

Review

Pages 40-41 Read each sentence. Add **ing** or **ed** to the word and write it on the line.

1. Everyone _____ when Mike got the award. (clap)
2. The rain is _____ off the roof. (drip)
3. A woodpecker is _____ on the tree bark. (tap)
4. We _____ the sticky jam off the floor. (mop)
5. Mom is busy _____ my sister's hair. (trim)
6. Pat _____ his sore elbow. (rub)
7. Two kangaroos are _____ in the tall grass. (hop)
8. The clerk _____ the tags on the dresses. (pin)

Pages 42-45 Read each word. Then write the word and add **s** or **es** to make it mean more than one.

seal _____   bush _____
bus _____   shark _____
stingray _____ coach _____
lunch _____   lion _____
zebra _____   glass _____
box _____   tiger _____

Pages 46-49 Draw a line to match the two words that go together to make a compound word. Then write the word on the line.

1. week   mother   _____
2. mail   end   _____
3. back   box   _____
4. grand   thing   _____
5. some   pack   _____
6. down   book   _____
7. note   room   _____
8. bed   town   _____

Pages 50-53 Write the correct word on the line.

meet - meat		I - eye
road - rode	for - four	write - right
our - hour	hear - here	see - sea

1. Do you _____ someone knocking at the door?
2. Mike and _____ are going to be in a play.
3. A ranger can _____ far from the lookout.
4. We must put on _____ coats before going outside.
5. Pete _____ his bike to the park.
6. I will sharpen my pencil before I _____ the letter.
7. We will _____ grandmother at the station.
8. Vern planted _____ apple trees in the yard.

Dont' Be Confused

Word List

would	away	guess
many	love	trouble
nice	every	nothing
any	party	goes

Use the Word List to unscramble the letters to spell a word. Write the word on the line.

1. o h i n n t g _____
2. l t e u o r b _____
3. s u s g e _____
4. a y a w _____
5. o g s e _____
6. i e c n _____
7. a y m n _____
8. e l v o _____
9. u w d l o _____
10. e e y v r _____
11. r p y t a _____
12. y n a _____

Write the three words above that you think are the hardest to spell.

_____ _____ _____

difficult words

Use the Word List to complete the puzzle.

Across
2. One or some
3. A celebration
7. Opposite of everything
9. All
11. Opposite of hate
12. Opposite of comes

Down
1. Several
4. Difficulty
5. Courteous and polite
6. Rhymes with say
8. Rhymes with mess
10. Homonym of wood

A Family Gathering

Write the word that names the person(s) in each picture.

1. _____
2. _____
3. _____
4. _____
5. _____
6. _____
7. _____
8. _____
9. _____
10. _____
11. _____
12. _____

"family" words

Read each clue. Write the correct words from page 58 on the lines. Then use the numbered letters to solve the code.

1. Another word for mom _ _ _ _ _ _
                                1
2. Dad's mother _ _ _ _ _ _ _ _ _
                         2
3. Mom's father _ _ _ _ _ _ _
                       3
4. Mom's sister _ _ _ _
                   4
5. Dad's brother _ _ _ _
                   5
6. Two persons from the same family born on the same day _ _ _ _ _
                                                           6   7
7. Opposite of girl _ _ _
                      8
8. A very small child _ _ _
                        9
9. Opposite of sister _ _ _ _ _ _
                           10
10. Another word for dad _ _ _ _ _
                          11
11. Opposite of boy _ _ _ _
                       12
12. Opposite of brother _ _ _ _ _
                         13

_ _ _ _ _ _ _ _
11 9 2 13 12 13 10 7

_ _ _
9 1 10

_ _ _ _ _ _ _ _ _ _ _ !
6 8 5 3 10 1 11 4 12

©1992 Instructional Fair, Inc.   59   IF0126 Spelling

A Circus of Colors

Word List

purple	red	black
tan	blue	gray
yellow	green	brown
pink	white	orange

Write the "color" words in alphabetical order.

1. _____
2. _____
3. _____
4. _____
5. _____
6. _____
7. _____
8. _____
9. _____
10. _____
11. _____
12. _____

Which color do you like most? _____
Which color do you like least? _____
What color is your favorite ice cream? _____
What color is your favorite fruit? _____
What color is your favorite chair? _____

"color" words

Use the code to color the picture.

1—pink
2—yellow
3—black
4—white
5—purple
6—tan
7—blue
8—red
9—gray
10—orange
11—brown
12—green

Use the picture to write the missing color words on the lines.

Herman and Clyde are clowns. Herman is the tall clown with _____ hair. Clyde is the short clown with _____ hair. Both of them have _____ noses. Herman always wears his old _____ shirt and _____ socks. He has to use _____ suspenders to hold up his big _____ pants. Clyde looks funny in his _____ and _____ polka-dotted costume. He says that his _____ hat is lucky. Clyde's feet are not as big as his _____ shoes. Would you like to have a _____ elephant balloon, too?

The Countdown Begins

Word List

one	two
three	four
five	six
seven	eight
nine	ten
plus equals minus	

Work the problems. Write the answers. Then write the answers using the correct number words.

1. 18 - 9 = ____   _____
2. 12 - 8 = ____   _____
3. 14 - 7 = ____   _____
4. 10 - 9 = ____   _____
5. 12 - 7 = ____   _____
6. 13 - 3 = ____   _____
7. 11 - 5 = ____   _____
8. 12 - 9 = ____   _____
9. 13 - 5 = ____   _____
10. 10 - 8 = ____   _____

Write the math problems using **only** words.

4 + 6 = 10   _____

8 - 3 = 5   _____

9 - 7 = 2   _____

1 + 5 = 6   _____

"number" words

This graph tells how many stars each person saw last night. Use the graph to answer the questions. Write the correct number word on the line.

Name											Number of Stars
Mandy	▓	▓	▓	▓	▓	▓	▓	▓			
Beth	▓	▓									
Ray	▓	▓	▓	▓							
Matt	▓	▓	▓	▓	▓	▓	▓	▓	▓	▓	
Darlene	▓										
Sam	▓	▓	▓	▓	▓	▓					
Andrea	▓	▓	▓								
Pete	▓	▓	▓	▓	▓						
Carl	▓	▓	▓	▓	▓	▓	▓	▓	▓		
Greta	▓	▓	▓	▓	▓	▓	▓				

How many more stars did...
    Mandy see than Beth? _____
    Carl see than Greta? _____
    Pete see than Ray? _____
    Sam see than Darlene? _____
    Matt see than Greta? _____

How many stars did these people see altogether?
    Pete and Beth _____
    Greta and Andrea _____
    Andrea and Darlene _____
    Pete and Ray _____
    Beth and Sam _____

Write the word for each symbol.
    = _____
    + _____
    − _____

Cool Choices

Read the name of each ice-cream flavor. Write the word from above that tells which choice it is.

1. cherry
2. lemon
3. vanilla
4. orange
5. blueberry
6. strawberry
7. rockyroad
8. chocolate
9. lime
10. butternut
11. pineapple
12. peach

"ordinal number" words

You decide! Write the ordinal number word to tell in what order you would choose each flavor.

1. blueberry
2. butternut
3. cherry
4. chocolate
5. lemon
6. lime
7. orange
8. peach
9. vanilla
10. rockyroad
11. strawberry
12. pineapple

Write the ordinal number word under each picture.

©1992 Instructional Fair, Inc.   IF0126 Spelling

What a Busy Day

Write the days of the week in the correct order.

1. _____
2. _____
3. _____
4. _____
5. _____
6. _____
7. _____

Read each clue. Write the correct word on the line.

1. The day before today   _____
2. This day   _____
3. Seven days make this.   _____
4. The day after today   _____
5. A week has seven of them.   _____

"calendar" words

Read the calendar. The days of the week are written in abbreviated form.

Sun.	Mon.	Tues.	Wed.	Thurs.	Fri.	Sat.
Visit Uncle Joe	Go to the bookstore	Go fishing	Baseball game	Skateboard contest	Help Mom clean house	Go to the beach

Use the calendar to write the missing word on the line. Write the whole word for each day of the week.

1. We will go fishing on _____.
2. On _____ we will be able to look for seashells.
3. We can buy two new books on _____.
4. We will have fun at Uncle Joe's farm on _____.
5. I hope our team wins the game on _____.
6. _____ morning we will be busy helping Mom.
7. Dad's buying us new skateboards for the contest this _____.
8. The calendar shows one whole _____.
9. If today is Friday, then _____ is Saturday.
10. The calendar shows all seven _____ of a week.
11. If today is Tuesday, then _____ was Monday.
12. If yesterday was Monday, then _____ is Tuesday.

'Tis the Season for Holidays

Word List

Valentine's Day   Easter
Halloween   summer
Christmas   fall
Fourth of July   St. Patrick's Day
New Year's Day   Thanksgiving
winter   spring

Read each clue. Write the correct holiday or season on the line. Remember to capitalize the first letter of a holiday.

1. You put on a costume. _____
2. First day of the year _____
3. Wear something green. _____
4. Fireworks in the sky _____
5. Time for presents _____
6. Hearts everywhere _____
7. Look for hidden eggs. _____
8. Give thanks. _____
9. Cold and snowy _____
10. Leaves change color. _____
11. Sunny and hot _____
12. Flowers bloom. _____

Write a sentence about your favorite holiday.

_____

_____

"calendar" words

Circle the misspelled words in each sentence and then write them correctly on the lines below.

1. Harvey helps rakes leaves in the fill.
2. On sts patrek dya Kelly found a four-leaf clover.
3. Last weentr Steve and I made a huge snow fort.
4. Every eestr we get a basket filled with eggs.
5. Our family decorated a tree for krismiss.
6. We had a party on nuw yeers dae.
7. Grandmother baked two pumpkin pies for our tankgivings dinner.
8. Last sumr we went camping at the lake.
9. My friend gave me a special heart on vuluntins dea.
10. We watch colorful fireworks every forth uv juli.
11. Bill wore a clown costume to the halowen party.
12. Carla and Mark plant a garden every speng.

1. _____   7. _____
2. _____   8. _____
3. _____   9. _____
4. _____ 10. _____
5. _____ 11. _____
6. _____ 12. _____

Review

Pages 56-57 Circle the correctly spelled missing word for each sentence.
1. Everyone had fun at the Halloween _____.
              parde   party
2. _____ you like to pet a giraffe?
              Would   Wood
3. What is the _____ with that computer?
              trouble   trubel
4. Can you _____ how many apples are in the basket?
              gess   guess

Pages 58-59 Unscramble the letters to spell words that name people in a family. Write the words on the lines.

roebrth _____   othmre _____
ncleu _____   rdganafhter _____
unat _____   gndrmaoethr _____
ahfetr _____   irsste _____
abyb _____   wntis _____

Pages 60-61 Write the best color words for each item.

ripe tomato _____   grape jam _____
banana _____   sky _____
elephant _____   pumpkin _____
twigs _____   plants _____
zebra _____   and _____

Pages 62-63 Work the problems. Circle the correct answer, and then write the correct number word.

1. 17 - 8 =   9   or   8   _____
2. 12 - 9 =   6   or   3   _____
3. 15 - 9 =   5   or   6   _____
4. 11 - 9 =   2   or   3   _____
5. 13 - 8 =   5   or   4   _____

Pages 64-65 Write the correct ordinal number words.

1st _____   7th _____
2nd _____   8th _____
3rd _____   9th _____

Pages 66-67 Write the days of the week in alphabetical order.

1. _____   5. _____
2. _____   6. _____
3. _____   7. _____
4. _____

Pages 68-69 Write the name of each holiday or season.

©1992 Instructional Fair, Inc.   IF0126 Spelling